NATIONAL
GEOGRAPHIC

The Home Front During
WORLD WAR II

BUY WAR BONDS

Monica Halpern

PICTURE CREDITS
Cover (background), 4, 6, 10, 11 (top), 14 (top), 17, 22 (bottom), 27
(bottom) Time Life Pictures/Getty Images; cover (inset), 1, 5, 8, 14
(bottom), 15, 18 Northwestern University Library Collection; border
(throughout), 34 (top) John Springer Collection/Corbis; pages 2–3,
9 (top), 20 (top), 29 (bottom), 30, 35, 36 (top and bottom), 38, 39
Bettmann/Corbis; pages 7, 29 (top), 33 Corbis; pages 9 (bottom), 21,
22 (top), 27 (top), 28, 31 (top), 32 (left), 37 AP Wide World Photos;
page 11 (left) Congressional Medal of Honor Society; page 11 (right)
Courtesy of David J. Devine; pages 12, 13, 20 (bottom), 23, 24–25,
26 Courtesy of the Library of Congress; page 16 Lake County
Museum/Corbis; page 19 FDR Library/National Archives; page 25
Courtesy of the National Archives; page 31 National Periodical
Publications, Inc.—D.C. Comics; page 32 (right) University of San
Diego Special Collections; page 34 (bottom) Getty Images.

QUOTATIONS
Page 4 John Bartlett, *Familiar Quotations*, (New York: Little, Brown, 1955),
p. 921; page 11 Norman Polmar and Thomas B. Allen, *World War II*
(New York: Random House, 1991), p. 157; page 12 Kawano, Kenji
Warriors, Navajo Code Talkers (Northland Publishing, 1990); page 21
Frank, Ziebarth & Field, *The Life and Times of Rosie the Riveter*, p. 23;
page 23 Maggi M. Morehouse, Fighting in the Jim Crow Army (Lanham,
Maryland: Rowman & Littlefield Pub., Inc., 2000), p. 8; page 27 A speech
to the Brotherhood of Sleeping Car Porters; page 32 Norman Polmar
and Thomas B. Allen, *World War II* (New York: Random House, 1991),
p. 533; page 38 Karen Zeinert, *Those Incredible Women of World War II*
(Brookfield, Conn.: The Millbrook Press, 1994), p. 95.

Produced through the worldwide resources of the National Geographic
Society, John M. Fahey, Jr., President and Chief Executive Officer;
Gilbert M. Grosvenor, Chairman of the Board; Nina D. Hoffman,
Executive Vice President and President, Books and Education
Publishing Group.

PREPARED BY NATIONAL GEOGRAPHIC SCHOOL PUBLISHING
Ericka Markman, Senior Vice President and President, Children's Books
and Education Publishing Group; Steve Mico, Vice President, Editorial
Director; Marianne Hiland, Executive Editor; Anita Schwartz, Project
Editor; Jim Hiscott, Design Manager; Kristin Hanneman, Illustrations
Manager; Diana Bourdrez, Picture Editor; Matt Wascavage, Manager of
Publishing Services; Sean Philpotts, Production Manager.

MANUFACTURING AND QUALITY MANAGEMENT
Christopher A. Liedel, Chief Financial Officer; Phillip L. Schlosser,
Director; Clifton M. Brown, Manager.

PROGRAM DEVELOPMENT Gare Thompson Associates, Inc.

ART DIRECTOR Dan Banks, Project Design Company

CONSULTANTS/REVIEWERS
Dr. Margit E. McGuire, School of Education, Seattle University,
Seattle, Washington

BOOK DEVELOPMENT Nieman, Inc.

BOOK DESIGN Three Communication Design, LLC

MAP DEVELOPMENT AND PRODUCTION Bruce Burdick

Published by the National Geographic Society
1145 17th Street, N.W.
Washington, D.C. 20036-4688

ISBN: 0-7922-4558-X

Printed in Canada

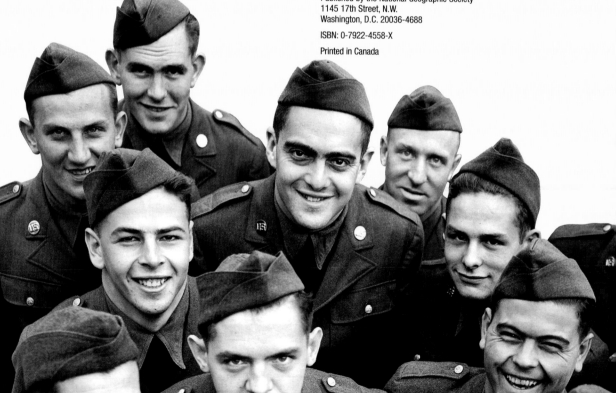

TABLE OF CONTENTS

"Yesterday, December 7, 1941—a date which will live in infamy—the United States of America was suddenly and deliberately attacked by naval and air forces of the Empire of Japan."

—PRESIDENT FRANKLIN D. ROOSEVELT, *war message to Congress*

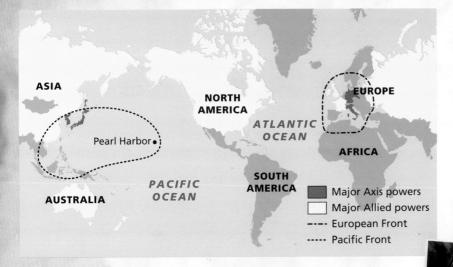

Major Axis powers
Major Allied powers
- - - - European Front
· · · · Pacific Front

Introduction

Sunday, December 7, 1941, dawned bright and sunny. Sunday was a day off for most officers, sailors, and soldiers stationed at the large base at Pearl Harbor in Hawaii. Eight battleships were anchored close together in the harbor. In nearby airfields, American airplanes were parked wing-to-wing. All was quiet.

Suddenly, dozens of Japanese bombers and fighter planes flew in fast and low. First, they struck the airfields. Their goal was to destroy as many U.S. airplanes as possible. At almost the same moment, Japanese bombers struck the battleships. The *Arizona* was the first to explode and sink. In the end, 19 ships were sunk or damaged. Hundreds of planes were destroyed on the ground. Some 2,400 people were killed.

The day after the Pearl Harbor attack, December 8, 1941, the United States declared war on Japan. Earlier, Japan had joined Germany and Italy in an alliance. They were called the Axis Powers. So, on December 11, the United States declared war on Germany and Italy too. The United States had joined what were known as the Allied Powers, or the Allies. They included Great Britain, France, and the Soviet Union. The United States had entered World War II on two fronts, the Pacific and the European.

America Goes to War

The United States was late in joining World War II. The war in Europe had actually started on September 1, 1939. The causes of the war had begun long before.

The 1930s were a hard time all over the world. Many countries were suffering from a worldwide depression, a severe decline in business. Germany was especially hard hit. Hoping to make things better, the Germans chose a new leader in 1933, Adolph Hitler.

Hitler was head of the National Socialist German Workers' party, called the Nazis. Once in power, Hitler became a dictator. He ruled by force. He wanted to make Germany a world power, so he began to add to Germany's territory. German troops took over Austria and Czechoslovakia in 1938. In 1939, they attacked and defeated Poland. Days later, on September 3, Britain and France declared war on Germany. They wanted to stop Hitler.

In the early 1930s, Japan was also in a depression. Military leaders rose to power. They promised to build a new Japanese empire. They began to attack other countries in Asia. Japan, Germany, and Italy, the Axis Powers, wanted to rule the world.

| With arm outstretched in a Nazi salute, Hitler inspects his troops.

The 1930s were a period in American history called the Great Depression. Banks failed. Factories closed. Many people lost their jobs. Some families no longer had a place to live.

When Franklin D. Roosevelt became President in 1932, he began to make changes. Slowly, the nation grew strong again. However, there was a still a lot to do in America. Many people did not want to take part in a war that seemed so far away.

Gradually, people changed their minds. Americans watched in horror as Germany quickly defeated Norway, Denmark, the Netherlands, Belgium, Luxembourg, and France. By the middle of 1940, Britain stood alone against Germany. German planes began to bomb cities, factories, and shipyards in Britain. Britain asked the United States for help. Roosevelt said he would supply the materials the British needed to fight the war.

German soldiers march through the streets of Poland after the Nazi invasion in 1939.

Roosevelt had a reason for wanting to send war materials to Britain. He believed that America was likely to enter the war very soon, and he wanted to get ready. Roosevelt had two goals. First, he wanted to make the nation's industries stronger. Second, he wanted to build up the armed forces.

So, even before the attack on Pearl Harbor, factories began to change what they produced. They turned out more ships, airplanes, ammunition, weapons, tanks, and other war materials. Workers produced more iron, steel, aluminum, and rubber. Then, Pearl Harbor was attacked. Within two weeks, Roosevelt began to tell factories what to make. For example, auto companies could no longer make cars. Instead, they began to make tanks, planes, and other military supplies.

The United States had also begun to raise an army before Pearl Harbor. Congress passed a new bill in 1940. It said that young men between the ages of 21 and 35 had to serve in the military. At first, some people were angry. After Pearl Harbor, young men rushed to join up. Some recruiting offices stayed open around the clock! In that first week after the bombing, nearly 25,000 men signed up.

Recruiting posters urged young men to join the armed forces.

OFF TO WAR

With the slogan "Remember Pearl Harbor!" ringing in their ears, the new soldiers went to war. Most were leaving home for the first time. Many found themselves living with people who were very different from them. Some soldiers could not read and write. Others had gone to college. Some came from homes without indoor plumbing or electricity. Others lived in mansions. Tough city boys shared housing with farm boys. Northerners bunked next to Southerners, although black and white troops were kept apart. Most people got along. Many made friends that would last a lifetime. By war's end, more than 15 million men and women had served in the armed forces.

Army recruits salute the flag in Mississippi in 1943.

MEET | Franklin Delano Roosevelt

Many believe that Franklin Delano Roosevelt was one of the greatest Presidents this country has ever had. He became President in 1932, in the middle of the Great Depression. He set the tone for his first term by telling Americans, "The only thing we have to fear is fear itself." His active, can-do approach helped put the nation back on track. Roosevelt was re-elected in 1936, 1940, and 1944. He was the only President to serve more than two terms. He led the country through World War II. Roosevelt died just weeks before the war ended.

9

Early in the war, few blacks were allowed to join the Air Force. Those who did join worked at low-level jobs. Under pressure from black leaders, the Army Air Force set up a flight-training center for blacks. It was located at Tuskegee Institute, a black college in Alabama. Some 1,000 black pilots were trained for combat here. They were called the "Tuskegee Airmen."

These pilots were officers, but they were barred from officers' clubs. They rode on segregated trains. When the trains were filled with white soldiers, the blacks had to sit on trunks in the baggage cars. The proud pilots called themselves the "Black Eagles." Bitter about how they were treated, they also called themselves the "Lonely Eagles."

Four of the 1,000 soldiers selected for flight training listen to an officer's instructions.

The first class graduated in March 1942. They sat around for over a year while the Army Air Force decided what to do with them. Finally, in April 1943, the all-black 99th Fighter Squadron was sent to join the war in North Africa. From then until the end of the war, the Tuskegee Airmen shot down 111 enemy planes.

LATINOS IN THE WAR

Between 250,000 and 500,000 Latinos served in the armed forces during World War II. More than 50,000 Puerto Rican men served. Two hundred Puerto Rican women served in the Women's Army Corps. Many Latinos were in the most dangerous branches, the paratroopers and the Marines. Latino soldiers were not segregated in the military the way black Americans were.

In the Pacific war, Latinos fought in the Philippine Islands. They were among those troops captured and imprisoned by the Japanese. Perhaps the most famous Latino unit was Company E of the 141st Infantry Regiment from Texas. Made up of mostly Spanish-speaking troops, the regiment fought in France and Italy. More than a thousand were killed. Members of the company received many decorations, including the Distinguished Service Cross. Of the 431 Medals of Honor awarded, Latinos earned 12. The Medal of Honor is awarded for bravery.

Paratroopers prepare for a jump.

(left) Medal of Honor (right) Distinguished Service Cross

Voices from America

"We fought two wars: one with the enemy and the other back home in the U.S.A."

—AN AFRICAN-AMERICAN PILOT

11

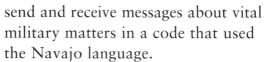

More than 40,000 Native Americans served in World War II. The Navajo code talkers are perhaps the best known. More than 500 Navajos were in the Marines. About 400 were trained to be code talkers in the Pacific. Their job was to send and receive messages about vital military matters in a code that used the Navajo language.

The Navajo language turned out to be perfect for developing a code. The language is unwritten and has several different forms. Except for a very few non-Navajos, only Navajos in the southwest United States speak the language. When the Japanese listened to the messages, they were mystified. They never broke the code.

A code talker listens for orders.

Voices from America

"When I was going to boarding school, the U.S. government told us not to speak Navajo, but during the war, they wanted us to speak it!"

—TEDDY DRAPER, SR., former Navajo code talker

Good Times, Bad Times

The war changed many things at home almost overnight. In lots of ways, people's lives got better fast. Factories were booming, and there were plenty of jobs. Farmers did much better too. Everyone in the war needed to be fed. So, prices for farm products went up. Just about everyone was making more money. Families were able to put in modern conveniences, such as running water and electric stoves. Many people could now go out to movies and restaurants. They could even buy luxuries, such as cameras and jewelry.

Although war brought unexpected good times, most people knew someone who was fighting in the war. Families lived in fear. They were afraid they would receive a telegram saying a loved one was killed or missing. As the war went on, people at home had to make sacrifices too.

Families were strongly encouraged to plant gardens and conserve resources.

13

Americans at home were far from the bombings and battles. Still, the war had a big effect on their lives. Many things were not available because they were needed for the war. As a result, some goods were rationed. That meant that people were given coupons that let them buy only a certain amount. Some rationed goods were sugar, butter, meat, coffee, gasoline, and tires.

A woman uses her ration stamps at a grocery store.

Stores were often out of rationed items. When hard-to-get goods came in, people stood in long lines to buy them. Families learned to make do. They made meatless sausage. They used coffee grounds over and over again to make a watery drink called "Roosevelt coffee." They planted "victory gardens" in any unused piece of soil. Here, they grew the vegetables they could not find in stores.

Some people bought hard-to-get goods on the black market. This term referred to any place where you could buy or sell goods illegally. Usually, prices were higher.

Most of the time, people found ways of living with the shortages. They remembered why they were making the sacrifice: to help the boys overseas.

1 Pound SUGAR ALLOWANCE COUPON 1 Pound
For Home Food Processing
OPA Form R-327

This coupon authorizes the holder to whom it was issued to receive 1 pound of sugar, which is to be used only to conserve fruit, fruit juices, or other foods as specified in the Regulations for the use of the person or persons listed on the Home Canning Sugar Application (Form No. R-323) or the Special Purpose Application (Form No. R-315) on file at the office of the Board indicated below.

914023 A

Serial Number of War Ration Book _____

Board No. _____ State _____

☆ GPO 16—33320-1

1 POUND

Families were allowed four pounds of sugar per month, which they bought with ration stamps.

14

FROM SCRAP DRIVES TO WAR BONDS

Many people wanted to do more to help the war effort. War factories were desperately short of raw materials. So, citizens joined in nationwide scrap drives. Children gave up their dolls and other toys made of rubber. They pulled red wagons around their neighborhoods, asking for scrap. They collected pots and pans, tin cans, car bumpers, and old bicycles. This scrap metal was then melted down to make planes, tanks, and guns. Children also gathered scrap paper. It was used to make food containers for the military. Even cooking grease was reused to make ammunition.

People also helped the war effort by loaning the government money. They did this by buying war bonds. The most common bond could be bought for $18.75. After ten years, the bond was worth $25. People could cash in bonds and receive the money.

School children bought war stamps for a dime or a quarter until they had enough to buy a war bond. Individual Americans bought billions of dollars worth of war bonds. Companies bought billions more. This money helped the American government pay for the war.

Making Scrap Count

- 1 tire = 12 gas masks
- 1 shovel = 4 hand grenades
- 1 lawn mower = 6 3-inch shells
- 1 radiator = 17 .30-caliber rifles

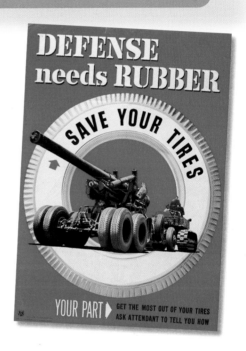

Posters encouraged saving scrap.

War changed daily life in many ways. People did not dress as they had before. Wool was needed for uniforms. So, to save cloth, men's three-piece suits became two-piece suits. They did not include a vest. Wool suits no longer had cuffs. Pleats were not allowed in men's or women's clothing because they took too much material. Women's stockings then were made of silk or nylon and had a dark seam down the back of the leg. However, parachutes were made of silk and nylon, and stockings became hard to get. When they ran out of stockings, women painted a seam down the backs of their bare legs.

Finding a place to live became a big problem. New factories needed many workers. People moved into factory towns to take jobs. Military bases brought in thousands of troops. Their wives and families often followed. Towns had many more people, but no new housing could be built. Building materials were being used for the war. So, local people rented out spare rooms, garages, sheds, and attics. Some desperate workers shared "hot beds" in rooming houses. They rented them for eight-hour sleeping shifts!

On the home front, rationing even affected men's fashions.

DEFENDING THE HOME FRONT

Food, clothing, and housing were not the only worries Americans at home had. The bombing of Pearl Harbor made them fear for their own safety. If the Japanese could attack Hawaii, could they reach the West Coast? Many thought a Japanese attack was likely. Also, German submarines were blowing up American ships sailing across the Atlantic Ocean. Many feared the Germans might soon invade America's East Coast.

Fearing an attack on U.S. soil, citizens participated in air-raid drills.

Volunteers helped keep America safe during the war.

Volunteers rushed to join a home defense group called the Civilian Defense Corps. They wore white metal helmets and armbands and carried gas masks. They patrolled their neighborhoods. Some volunteers made sure people covered their windows completely at night. Lights would show enemy pilots where to go. Other workers stared at the skies looking for enemy airplanes. There were more than a million spotters. Not one ever saw an enemy plane.

Women in the War

After the attack on Pearl Harbor, women found their own way of helping the war effort. Factories were hiring every man who had not gone off to fight. Yet, they were still short of workers. So, women stepped forward to do their part as "production soldiers."

Before the war, most women never expected to work outside the home. Only about a quarter of the workers in America were women. Most of them were nurses, teachers, and social workers. In the five months after Pearl Harbor, some 750,000 women volunteered for jobs at war plants. At first, factory managers were slow to hire them. By the end of the war, about one-third of all workers were women.

About five million women went to work for the first time during the war. Some were housewives who had never worked outside the home. Others were young women just out of high school. They were white, black, and Latinos. They were school dropouts and college graduates.

Women joined the defense industry by the thousands.

Women took over jobs in many industries, including defense, previously held by men.

ROSIE THE RIVETER

Women did many jobs formerly done by men. They learned to weld and **rivet** and operate big cranes. They put together guns and ships. Women drove trucks, trains, and tractors. They worked through wind, rain, snow, cold, and heat. They got used to the earsplitting noise of heavy machinery. They learned to live with the dirt and the danger.

The best-known war job for women was riveter. These women built airplanes by shooting rivets, or metal bolts, into metal parts. In some aircraft plants, one out of every three workers was a woman. "Rosie the Riveter" came to stand for all the women who took on tough jobs for the war effort. She appeared in songs, posters, films, and magazine covers. Rosie was a war hero.

Rosie the Riveter was on a magazine cover during the war.

Women discovered that working in a factory was not easy. At first, many had to put up with insults from the men they worked with. They were called "lipsticks" or "dollies." In time, however, their hard work won over most male workers. Their patience, eagerness to learn, and outstanding results greatly impressed their managers.

Women factory workers had to change the way they dressed. They had never worn anything but skirts. Now, many of them had to dress like men. For safety, they wore slacks or overalls, heavy shoes, and thick gloves to work. They cut their hair short or wore it tied up in a scarf.

Voices from America

"When we finished one of these beautiful ships, it was an inspiring, thrilling thing."

—A FEMALE SHIPBUILDER

Some women worked up to 70 hours a week. They made good money, although usually less than men for the same jobs. Most women were working to help win the war. They also took pride in their new skills. They liked earning their own money. Many were living independent lives for the first time.

Women assemble jeeps in Michigan.

21

WOMEN IN THE MILITARY

**Pilots line up
for review**

Some women wanted to help win the war by joining the military. At first, the government would not let women serve, and the military did not want them. Then, in May 1942, the first women were allowed to join the army. On that day, more than 13,000 women rushed to recruiting stations around the country to sign up for the Women's Auxiliary Army Corps (WAAC).

That same year, other women's units were formed: the WASPS (Women Air Force Service Pilots), the navy WAVES (Women Accepted for Volunteer Emergency Services), and the coast guard SPARS. More than 60,000 army and navy nurses also served, some of them overseas. More than 275,000 women volunteered for military service. These women won the praise and respect of the male generals who had once doubted they could do the job.

MEET | Jacqueline Cochran

Jacqueline Cochran received her pilot's license in 1932. At the beginning of the war, she ferried U.S. bombers to England. She then organized and became director of the WASPS. She was awarded the Distinguished Service Medal in 1945. In 1953, Cochran became the first woman to break the sound barrier.

Relocation and Racial Unrest

World War II was fought to protect people's rights to democracy and freedom around the world. Yet, some groups at home in America did not have these rights. When the war started, African Americans lived segregated lives. More than three-quarters of them lived in the South. About half of them lived on farms. Most were poor. Jobs were hard to get. Still, most wanted to serve their country. They also believed that the military would give them steady work and better job opportunities. Also, some were hoping for adventure.

Some black leaders called for black soldiers to fight for victory at home as well as victory abroad. This was called the "Double V" campaign. Many blacks hoped that by helping to win the war they would change things for African Americans at home. They hoped blacks would gain improved rights.

A man pickets for work in Chicago.

Voices from America

"If we went in and proved ourselves, they would have to say, 'Hey, look. These people are A-number-1, so we'll have to treat them as citizens.'"

—AN AFRICAN-AMERICAN SOLDIER

23

One group of Americans was treated especially badly during the war. About 120,000 Japanese Americans lived in the United States at the start of the war. Nearly all lived in the states of Washington, Oregon, and California. Two-thirds of them were American citizens. More than one-fourth were children under age 15.

After Pearl Harbor, many people thought all Japanese were the enemy. They believed that Japanese Americans would not be loyal to America. In February 1942, President Roosevelt signed an order saying that Japanese Americans could be forced to leave their homes. They were to be taken to ten "relocation" camps. These camps were in remote areas far away from the coasts.

That spring, Japanese families received one week's notice to close up their businesses and homes. Families and shop owners held going-out-of-business sales. They gave away their pets. They took what clothing they could carry and waited for soldiers to take them to their new homes. About 110,000 people were moved to the camps.

The Manzanar Relocation Camp in California covered 500 acres.

LIFE IN THE CAMPS

Frightened Japanese-American families arrived at the camps not knowing what to expect. They were horrified at what they found. Each camp was made up of hundreds of buildings lined up in rows. Barbed wire surrounded the camps. Soldiers stood guard. Floodlights swept the grounds through the night.

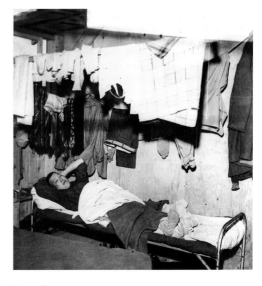

A family of four lived in a single room. They had no closets, shelves, or furniture other than cots and stoves for heat. There was no privacy. People shared bathrooms and shower rooms. Cooking was not possible in the crowded rooms. People ate together in a large dining hall. Children went to schools that were short of teachers, books, and classrooms.

The barracks at Manzanar did not have closets, so this man hung his clothes over his bed.

By 1943, the army needed more soldiers. So, it allowed Japanese Americans to enlist. Many did. More than 17,000 Japanese Americans fought for the United States during the war. They left their families behind in the camps. The 442nd Combat Team was formed entirely of Japanese Americans. Fighting in Italy, the 442nd became the most decorated military unit in U.S. history.

In 1988, the U.S. government made a public apology to the 60,000 victims of the camps who were still living. They paid each of them $20,000.

Black sailors had segregated quarters on their ship.

WE'RE IN THE ARMY NOW

Blacks joined a military that was segregated, just like the rest of America. Before World War II, the government thought about how best to use black soldiers. The decision was made to keep them in segregated units and in support positions. Black soldiers would not have the chance to fight in combat units.

Black units were supposed to be treated the same as white units, but they were not. Housing for black troops was usually poor. They had very limited chances for promotion. Black officers could command only black troops. Usually, white officers were put in charge of black troops.

The number of blacks in the military was carefully limited. The army used the percentage of young black males in the U.S. population as a yardstick. That meant that only ten percent of the army could be black. Also, black men could only be assigned to an all-black unit. There were just six of these. This rule kept many black men out of the army.

OPENING UP JOBS FOR BLACKS

The war brought opportunity to many African Americans, although they had to fight for it. Factories had expanded. Still, managers rarely hired blacks for anything but unskilled jobs. A. Philip Randolph was an important black leader. He planned a huge march to Washington to protest the lack of jobs for blacks in the defense industries. President Roosevelt heard of the plan. He didn't want the march to happen. First Lady Eleanor Roosevelt met with Randolph to see what it would take to stop the march. The answer, the President decided, was to set up the Fair Employment Practices Committee. This group's job was to see that all workers had an equal chance to get any job.

A National Guardsman keeps the peace on a bus during the transit strike.

Although some factories began to hire a few blacks, there were problems. Many white workers did not want to work with blacks. In 1944, the local trolley company in Philadelphia decided to hire its first eight black drivers. Protesting white drivers went out on strike. They shut down the city's entire public-transportation system. President Roosevelt called in 8,000 soldiers to break the strike. They kept the buses and trolleys running, and the black drivers kept their jobs.

Voices from America

"It is only within the framework of democracy that labor and minorities can achieve freedom, equality, and justice."

—A. PHILIP RANDOLPH

27

Detroit was a center of wartime production. Many workers were needed. However, the African Americans who moved there found big problems. There was not enough housing, and local white people did not want to live with blacks. In 1942, a new housing project was built in a white neighborhood. The following year, 20 black families tried to move in. A mob of 700 whites stopped the moving vans. Police broke up the riot, but they arrested young blacks instead of the rioting whites. Finally, two months later, state troopers helped the black families move in.

Other cities had race riots too. In the summer of 1943, wartime race riots reached their peak. Violence broke out in many cities. In Detroit, 25 blacks and 9 whites were killed.

THE ZOOT SUIT RIOTS

During a hot June week in 1943, white sailors roamed the streets of East Los Angeles. The sailors were dressed in uniform. They were about to go off to war. They were looking for young Mexican men dressed in zoot suits.

The zoot-suiters looked different. They wore long jackets with padded shoulders. They wore balloon pants. They carried a pocket watch on a long chain and wore a large, wide-brimmed hat. Their hair was long and slicked back in a ducktail.

The sailors found the young Mexicans foreign and odd. They thought zoot-suiters were **draft dodgers** and unpatriotic. The sailors attacked the young Mexicans. They ripped their clothes and cut their hair.

To stop the riots, the navy said sailors could not go to certain parts of Los Angeles. The city council made wearing a zoot suit a crime.

Zoot-suiter

28

This Is Your War

Every morning during the war, the first thing people did was read the newspaper. They were hungry for news. Their sons, husbands, fathers, and sometimes their wives and daughters were away at war. Family members at home followed events closely.

World War II reached a new high in news coverage. There were at least 500 war correspondents, reporters who wrote about the events of the war. That was five times more than in World War I.

Perhaps the best-known war correspondent was Ernie Pyle. His columns were published six times a week in hundreds of newspapers. He wrote chatty stories about the lives of ordinary soldiers. He called them "brave men." Families read his stories to get a sense of what their boys were going through.

| Ernie Pyle

"All the News That's Fit to Print."

The New York Times.

LATE

Copyright, 1941, by The New York Times Company.

THREE CENTS

VOL. XCI. No. 30,688.

NEW YORK, FRIDAY, DECEMBER 12, 1941.

U.S. NOW AT WAR WITH GERMANY AND ITALY; JAPANESE CHECKED IN ALL LAND FIGHTING; 3 OF THEIR SHIPS SUNK, 2D BATTLESHIP HIT

BLOCKED IN LUZON

But Japanese Put Small Force Ashore in South of Philippine Island

SABOTEURS ARE HELD

Some in Manila Seized for Spreading Rumor About City Water

Line-Up of World War II

THE ALLIES

Australia · Haiti
Belgium · Honduras
Canada · India
China · New Zealand
Costa Rica · Nicaragua
Cuba · (Czecho-Slovakia) (Norway)
Dominican · *Panama
Republic · †Poland
*El Salvador · South Africa
Free France · Soviet Union
Great Britain · United States
†Greece · †Yugoslavia
Guatemala

THE AXIS

Finland · Japan
Germany · Manchukuo
Hungary · Rumania
Italy · Slovakia

*Have declared war on Japan only.
†At war only with Germany, Italy and their European allies.

CITY CALM AND GRIM AS THE WAR WIDENS

Loyalty and a Determination to Win Are Evident in Every Class and National Group

U. S. FLIERS SCORE

Bombs Send Battleship, Cruiser and Destroyer to the Bottom

MARINES KEEP WAKE

Small Force Fights Off Foe Despite Loss of Some of Planes

Left: The President set his signature to the act against Germany. Center: He checked the time with Senator Tom Connally. Right: After that he placed the United States officially at war with Italy.

AXIS TO GET LESSON, CHURCHILL WARNS

He Announces Replacement of Libyan General—Upholds Phillips's Judgment

Our Declaration of War

The President's Message

WAR OPENED ON US

Congress Acts Quickly as President Meets Hitler Challenge

A GRIM UNANIMITY

Message Warns Nation Foes Aim to Enslave This Hemisphere

CONGRESS KILLS BAN ON AN A.E.F.

Swift Action Without Debate— Service Terms Are Extended to Six Months After War

29

RADIO

President Roosevelt often spoke to the nation.

People at home got their information in new ways in this war. Radio had taken over America's living rooms. Families sat around the radio every evening for entertainment and news. Radio brought world events to people faster and more dramatically than ever before. Radio described history as it was happening.

Voices from America

"Never before have we had so little time in which to do so much."

—PRESIDENT FRANKLIN ROOSEVELT, from his fireside chat, February 23, 1942

Franklin Roosevelt was the first President to use the radio as a tool. He used it to talk directly to the American people. An excellent speaker, Roosevelt held many radio news conferences. He also gave informal talks over the radio. They were called "fireside chats." He spoke simply and plainly to Americans about important issues. Listeners felt as though they were having a personal conversation with him. These talks helped him win their support.

"THIS IS LONDON"

The power of radio was demonstrated by the live broadcasts of correspondent Edward R. Murrow. In late 1940, Murrow broadcast daily reports from London rooftops. He began his broadcast with, "This . . . is London." He told what was happening to ordinary British people as German bombs fell on their city. Millions of Americans listened breathlessly to the roar of attacking airplanes. They heard the whistling of falling bombs and their explosions. Over it all, was Murrow's calm, deep voice. His reports made Americans want to help the British in the war.

| Edward R. Murrow

THE FUNNIES GO TO WAR

Comic books and newspaper "funnies" went to war before America did. The 1940s were the golden age of superheroes. Superman first appeared in 1938. He was followed by Batman, Aquaman, Wonder Woman, Captain Marvel, and other heroes with special powers. Many of these characters fought in the war, but not Superman. The publisher thought it would mock the war effort to show Superman fighting the war.

| Superman fought on the home front.

After all, with his special powers, Superman would have been able to win the war all by himself! So, Superman failed his eye test when he accidentally used his X-ray vision to read the eye chart in the next room.

The comics' hero Captain America wore a red, white, and blue, star-studded costume to fight the Nazis. Children who joined Captain America's Club had to promise to collect scrap for the war effort. In 1940, Joe Palooka, boxing hero of his own comic strip, joined the army. Many young men joined up as a result. President Roosevelt personally thanked the cartoonist, Ham Fisher.

"Fresh, spirited American troops, flushed with victory, are bringing in thousands of hungry, ragged, battle-weary prisoners."

"She Says the Government Can Have Her Zipper, If the Government Can Get It Un-jammed!"

SCRAP FOR VICTORY

Dr. Seuss Copyright 1942 Field Publications

Cartoonists such as Bill Mauldin and Dr. Seuss used humor to educate the public about the war.

CARTOONS

Cartoons have never been only for children. Newspapers and magazines carried many war-related cartoons. The artists used their cartoons to comment on the events of the war. Some of them made fun of war-related problems at home.

Bill Mauldin, an Army sergeant, was probably the most famous cartoonist of the war. He drew his cartoons, called "Up Front with Mauldin," for the army newspaper *Stars and Stripes*. His two main characters were Willie and Joe. They were footsore, unshaven soldiers who were tired of the war. Mauldin used them to stand for the soldiers he met on the battlefields of Europe.

Voices from America

"I draw pictures for and about the infantry because I know what their life is like. They don't get fancy pay and their food is the worst in the army because you can't whip up lemon pies or even hot soup at the front."

—BILL MAULDIN

Waiting for Victory

Americans were certain the Allies would win the war, but they knew the cost in lives would be heavy. They looked for ways to take their minds off the war. For the first time in years, just about everyone was working. Most had extra money. They wanted to have fun. They needed to laugh. They wanted to feel patriotic.

People read more than ever. For the first time, they could buy books in paperback. The books cost only a quarter. So, more people bought books. They read mysteries, westerns, and, of course, war stories.

Americans listened to all kinds of music too. Big bands, such as Duke Ellington's, played popular songs that kept young people dancing and singing through the war. All-girl singing groups were popular too. The Andrews Sisters' recording of "Boogie-Woogie Bugle Boy" was one of the biggest hits of the war.

The Andrews Sisters sing for an audience of sailors.

A tense moment
in the movie
Air Force

LET'S GO TO THE MOVIES

It seemed as if everyone went to the movies. During the first 6 months of the war, more than 70 war-related films were released. They were shown to make people feel patriotic. Viewers left the theater believing that their nation was right in going to war. Movies showed that everyone needed to give up things to win the war. In the movies, the good guys always won. Studios made comedies and lighthearted musicals too. People laughed and forgot their worries.

Getting into the movies cost a dime, or a quarter on weekends. Usually, moviegoers would see a double feature, two movies for the price of one. They also saw one or more cartoons. One popular extra was the newsreel. A newsreel was a short movie that showed current events, both at home and at war. Some theaters showed nothing but newsreels during the war. Before television, they were an important way for people to see war events. They helped moviegoers feel closer to their loved ones far from home.

THE USO

Soldiers needed to take their minds off the war too. So, early in the war, the United Service Organizations (USO) was formed to entertain members of the armed forces. Men and women in the armed forces away from home went to USO clubs. They could see a movie or go to a dance. They could eat a hot meal. They could find a quiet place to write a letter.

The USO also held shows in combat areas overseas. Hollywood stars, singers, comics, and musicians entertained the troops. They called themselves "soldiers in greasepaint." Comedian Bob Hope led the first of these tours in 1942. It was so successful that the army and navy asked him to go out again and again. He and his troupe performed for the rest of the war on bases and aboard warships. Sometimes, the performers got close enough to the action to hear gunfire.

Bob Hope entertaining the troops

TAKE ME OUT TO THE BALL GAME!

When many Major League players, such as Joe DiMaggio (top), went to war, the women's professional league helped keep baseball going.

The war changed America's national pastime, baseball. In 1941, Yankee slugger Joe DiMaggio hit in a record 56 straight games. A year later, he and many other star players were serving in the military. Baseball was so important to American morale that President Roosevelt allowed it to continue during the war.

As a result, some surprising players joined the major leagues. Joe Nuxhall was the youngest-ever major league baseball player at the age of 15! He was a pitcher for the Cincinnati Reds. The St. Louis Browns had a one-armed fielder, Pete Gray.

With so many men gone, baseball owners came up with a new idea, a women's professional league. The All-American Girls Professional Baseball League was started in 1943. The players had to follow special rules. They had to wear dresses and makeup on the field. At night, they had to go to charm school. Fans were amazed at how well the women played ball. League games drew big crowds.

VICTORY AT LAST

The war ended in Europe in May 1945. Japan surrendered in August. The Allies had won. Joyful crowds gathered everywhere to celebrate.

The seven million troops still overseas were rushed home. They were thrilled to be back in the United States. Getting used to life after the war was not easy. Women at home had been making all their own decisions. Children no longer knew their fathers. Housing was scarce. Until factories changed over from making war materials, jobs were hard to find.

Soon, however, factories were producing the everyday goods that people wanted. There were plenty of jobs. People had more money than ever before. Reunited families began a "baby boom." Many families were able to buy their own homes. They could afford to buy kitchen appliances and even the new television sets.

Returning soldiers had another great benefit, the G.I. Bill of Rights. It gave them loans to buy homes or start businesses. It also helped nearly eight million people go to college or trade school.

Crowds gathered in Times Square on VJ Day, August 14, 1945.

The end of war did not bring better times for everyone. Almost five million women lost their jobs to men coming back from war. Women were urged to go back home. Even so, there were still more working women than before the war. By 1948, their numbers began to grow again. Women had proved that they could do just about any job men could do.

Voices from America

"One afternoon just before the war ended, they laid off 108 of us. You never heard so many women crying in all your life."

—ADA HABERMEHL, factory worker

The war had opened up new opportunities for black men and women. Many had moved from the South to take new jobs in the North and West. Black veterans returned from war determined to make things better at home. They had fought for their country. They now expected to be treated with respect. Black veterans used the G.I. Bill to complete their education or buy a home. Many led the fight for equality. Things began to change for the better, but very slowly.

The war had made America a richer, more powerful nation than ever before. The next few years would be a time of peace and prosperity for most Americans.

Celebrating the war's end

alliance a formal agreement between countries to come to one another's aid in times of need

black market the illegal buying and selling of rationed goods or the place where these activities happened.

bond a certificate issued by a government that promises to pay back with interest the money paid for the bond

depression a period of economic hardship

dictator a person who rules with complete authority

draft dodger a person who tries to avoid the draft; the draft is the system of requiring people to serve as soldiers.

empire a group of countries or states under one ruler

front an area of military operations

morale the state of the spirits of a person or group of people; a person with good morale is confident and cheerful.

paratrooper a soldier trained to use a parachute to go down into a battle area

rationed given out in small, fixed amounts

rivet to fasten with a rivet, or metal bolt

scrap cast-off or worn-out material that can be turned into something new

segregated separated by racial groups

veteran a person who has served in the armed forces

war correspondent a journalist who reports from a place of battle

First Lady Eleanor Roosevelt delivering a radio broadcast in 1942

Index